Patterns
for Educational
Growth

Six Discourses

at the University of Notre Dame

by THEODORE M. HESBURGH, C.S.C.

President

1952 - 1958

University of Notre Dame Press
1958

IMPRIMI POTEST: Theodore J. Mehling, C.S.C.
Provincial

NIHIL OBSTAT: Charles E. Sheedy, C.S.C., S.T.D.
Censor Deputatus

IMPRIMATUR: ✠ Leo A. Pursley, D.D.
Bishop of Fort Wayne

February 18, 1958

AFFECTIONATELY DEDICATED

TO THE FACULTY

AT THE

UNIVERSITY OF NOTRE DAME

Contents

Introduction

IT HAS OFTEN SEEMED TO ME during these past six years that
a university President is always, and perhaps *ex officio*, in danger
of becoming illiterate. His opportunity to read and to write are
in inverse ratio to his necessity of speaking frequently, often
without advance warning, on a vast variety of subjects. Immediately upon his appointment, the public expects the university
President to be an authority on all things knowable. I have
orated during the past six years on athletics and astrophysics,
on juvenile delinquency and gnotobiotics, on marriage and
atoms for peace, on business, theology, education in South
America, and jet airplanes. These are only a few of the variegated
subjects upon which I have unburdened myself with words of
questionable wisdom. And yet, I can only plead that the force
of circumstances left me no alternative. It was a matter of
speak or disgrace my position. How often I have hoped against
hope that in speaking I did not disgrace myself. How frequently
I remembered the words of Mark Twain: "Better to be silent
and to be suspected of being ignorant, than to speak and thus
to remove all doubt."

However, once a year I had the opportunity of speaking upon
a subject that was germane to my essential hopes and activities
as President. At the beginning of each school year at Notre
Dame, I had the opportunity of speaking to our assembled
faculty at the inaugural Mass on some pertinent aspects of

university education. There was no set pattern to these discourses. I can only generalize that the more I understood the magnitude of the task at hand, the more difficult it became to write something that seemed even slightly adequate to that task. It is a personal impression that, although the talks became more difficult to write, they probably became better, or at least more significant, as the six years passed. I hope this is so. If not, then I did not learn very much from the experience of the six years.

Taken as a whole, these six discourses on different aspects of university education express the guiding lines of our educational endeavor at Notre Dame. They should convey some sense of the constant effort at self-examination that is the price of growing excellence in an educational institution — or any other institution for that matter. These discourses should reflect the constant striving for quality of performance, for a sense of what good has been accomplished and what heights may still be reached at Notre Dame. They speak insistently of the adequacy of knowledge that must be our aim in a Catholic university, of the wisdom that must be all-pervading, of the inner dignity and eternal worth of the educators effort, of the effects that may be hoped for in our students.

No doubt, the more sophisticated will find in these discourses a rather undisguised attempt on my part to inspire the faculty in the task that faces them anew each year. For this, I cannot apologize, because I happen to believe that a President who cannot inspire his faculty is not worth his salt. Of course, actual inspiration and the attempt to inspire are, unfortunately, not the same thing. The years ahead will know best, from the educational results of the faculty's efforts, whether or not their performance was actually inspired during these years. And if their work was inspired, I am sure that much more than these discourses was responsible for that inspiration.

Presenting these discourses to a wider public than our faculty may well be presumptuous on my part. However, our university has been the recipient of so much enlightened interest and help from such a multitude of people during these past years, that we feel some responsibility to report to this wider public regarding our program for a growing measure of educational excellence that will justify their interest and demonstrate the effectiveness of the help we have received from them. The ultimate accounting of effectiveness is most often given by statistics. The figures are indeed impressive. We have, during the past six years, completed sixteen million dollars worth of academic and auxiliary buildings. Our annual budget has grown from eight to fifteen million dollars. Our graduates have won more national and international scholarships during these past six years than in our whole previous history of more than a hundred years. We have completely revised the curriculum in most of our colleges, and have added many distinguished professors to our faculty.

Underlying these and other statistics that could be presented, there is the more important plan of action, or pattern for quality that provides the inner spirit of growth at Notre Dame. It is this inner plan or vision, the dynamic relating of the University to the key educational problems and opportunities of our day, that these discourses purport to give. In the realization of this overall plan, it is the faculty, not the President, which is most important. Perhaps then, the best title of these discourses would be "A President Dreams Aloud to his Faculty." It is my hope, shared alike by our many friends I am sure, that our faculty at Notre Dame will make all of these dreams come true in the life and growth of the University.

PATTERNS FOR EDUCATIONAL GROWTH

1 9 5 2

Wisdom

and Education

FOLLOWING a long and fruitful tradition, we gather here in Sacred Heart Church this morning for the eightieth time since the Church was built in 1871, to open, officially and formally, the 111th schoolyear of the University. As is the custom on these solemn occasions, we are offering together a Mass to the Holy Spirit to seek the wisdom and the courage demanded by the times, and expected of each one of us who have dedicated ourselves to Christian education of young men.

In seeking a theme this year, I have been led to apply to the University and its task today the celebrated motif of Arnold Toynbee's *Study of History*. As you know, Toynbee uses the ideas of challenge and response as his yardstick to measure the growth and decline of classical civilizations.

Every great civilization grew out of a challenge. Insofar as its response to the challenge was vital, the particular civilization grew and prospered. To the extent that it failed to meet the continuing challenge, each civilization in turn declined until today we find only in the pages of history, and on the carved surfaces of monuments, the glories of most classical cultures, now long since deceased.

Many have said that Western culture is dying; certainly, most will admit that it has lost much of its vitality. Yet it is precisely as a part of this rich heritage that we do survive. Not only a remnant are we, but a remnant linked with the spiritual tap-roots that have accounted for most of the vitality that has remained in Western culture.

3

Certainly it is fitting this year to review our part in
that rich pattern, the challenges that have been answered
and those that must yet be answered, if we are to con-
tribute our share to the survival of the larger reality of
Western culture, of which we are but a part.

The challenges that have faced great civilizations were
normally dual in character: physical challenges and
spiritual challenges. For example, the great Egyptian
civilization met the physical challenge of survival by
changing broad miasmic swamp lands into the fertile
valley of the Nile. But the Pharaohs failed in the larger
spiritual challenge of bringing social justice to their
people. It was the work of slaves, not free men, that
built the pyramids. Little did the rulers realize that they
were not only building magnificent tombs for themselves,
but for their civilization as well.

We have seen the ebb and flow of physical and spiritual challenges in this country as well as in this University. The pioneers conquered the West, the railroads
spanned the great continental plains, bridged the rivers,
and crossed the Rockies. Technology completed the task
so that today we race the sun across the land, and talk
from coast-to-coast as easily as from room-to-room. Yes,
the physical challenge of survival, the additional challenges of space and time have been met, but what of the
deeper challenges of the spirit?

Do Americans think better, read better, write better
today? Do they have a better married and family life, are
wars diminishing and prayers more fervent, are lives
more righteous in the sight of God? Or is God even
granted sight?

We know that our history here at the University, in
the light of the physical challenges of survival, paralleled
that of our country. One hundred and ten years ago,

Father Sorin arrived here after more than a week's arduous journey from nearby Vincennes, Indiana. His total assets were some bleak land, a drafty log cabin, an ox-cart full of goods, and less than $400 in cash. More important, no doubt, even in meeting the physical challenges, were the consecrated lives of his companions, the vision of faith, hope, and charity in his own stalwart heart.

He had more than his share of pestilence and plague, fire and drought, disappointments and deaths in those early years. But he made a vital response to each challenge, he grew with America, and added to the strong fiber of this country's growth.

Today we calculate the physical assets of Notre Dame in millions of dollars, the buildings at more than fifty, the manpower at fifteen hundred, the inventory in yard-long sheets of green I.B.M. inventory records. Yes, the physical challenges to the University, like those to our country, have been met with an adequate, and even an impressive response. But like the Egyptians of old, we cannot survive by merely building monuments. The lasting works of man are those of the spirit. Without them, monuments are never better than tombs.

What are the challenges of the spirit that face our civilization, our country, and our University today? Certainly, a prime challenge is the need for wisdom, not merely the pragmatic prudence of day-by-day decisions, but the age-old Christian wisdom that understands the whole pattern of creation and man's place in this pattern. Our work is the perfecting of human beings, drawing out and developing all the human potentialities of our students. Certainly this requires of us as educators some clear concept of what is good for men, for his body and for his soul, for his mind and his will, for only what is good for man will perfect man and assure him of the good life.

It is the work of wisdom to recognize the true human perfections and to order them rightly, so that we do not place the goods of the body above those of the soul, those of time against those of eternity. Wisdom gives us a pattern of ordered education, because it gives us an ordered view of the world and of man.

This Christian wisdom which begins with God, embraces man, and leads back to God, is the antithesis of the many current forms of wisdom, be they earthly in their total intent, sensual in their feverish pursuit, or satanical in their blind pride. Our prayer today is for the grace to ascend above these counterfeit forms of wisdom that can only lead to disorder, unhappiness, and frustration, because they begin with a false notion of man and then attempt to remake man according to that caricature. May our prayer for wisdom in the Mass today be accompanied by prayerful meditation on St. James' words, which reflect so well the fact that true wisdom in perfecting the mind of man leads to charity, peace, and order which characterize the perfection of man's will.

St. James states it thus:

Does any of you lay claim to wisdom or learning? Then let him give proof of his quality by setting a good example, living peaceably as a wise man should. As long as you find bitter jealousy and thoughts of rivalry in your hearts, let us have none of this boasting that perverts the truth; such wisdom as yours does not come from above, it belongs to earth and to nature, and is fit only for devils. Where there is jealousy, where there is rivalry, there you will find disorder and every kind of defeat. Whereas the wisdom which does come from above is marked chiefly indeed by its purity, but also by its peacefulness; it is courteous and ready to be convinced, always taking the better part; it carries mercy with it, and a harvest of all that is good; it is uncensorious, and without affectation. Peace is the seed-ground of holiness, and those who make peace will win its harvest (James iii. 13-18).

This Christian wisdom for which we pray today should be the hallmark of our profession. Our total educative process cannot lead those whom we educate to wisdom unless we begin by seeking to be wise ourselves, and to grow continually in wisdom. We cannot have too much wisdom, any more than we can have too much life or holiness. Nor is wisdom ever misused. A man may put artistic skill or scientific knowledge to evil use, but no man is truly wise unless he acts wisely.

It may occur to you that this emphasis on wisdom depreciates the many other kinds of artistic, technical, and professional knowledge that our University imparts. Yet this is no more true than to say that a recognition of the Supreme Being of God involves a denial of all the other myriad forms of being.

All other forms of knowledge can be ordered and hierarchically arranged under the highest knowledge called wisdom. In fact, without wisdom, and considered only in themselves, all other forms of knowledge and science run the risk of being distorted, simply because, without wisdom they are unrelated to everything else that is and, especially, because without wisdom they are unrelated to God, who supremely *IS*.

How important then that no matter what our branch of learning we seek first and foremost to be wise. The tragedy today is that so many educators are learned without being wise — or even good.

In praying for the divine gift of wisdom, we are asking for the fullness of truth, for while individual branches of learning may tend to disintegrate the totality of knowledge, wisdom unites all that is true, each in its proper proportion and perspective.

While the imparting of universal knowledge is the specific function of the University, yet we have ever been interested here in the total perfection of our students. Knowledge does not exist in a vacuum, but in a person who lives and moves and acts. A person's isolated and unrelated knowledge of specific facts may remain sterile, but wisdom leads a man to face the hurly-burly task of daily living with the peaceful and calm assurance of where he is going, and of the way of attaining the ultimate goals. This is why we do not call a man wise merely because he is learned in this or that field. To know wisely, is to know all that one knows in proper order and perspective. To be educated in this wisdom is to know how and why to love God. We who presume to educate young men could not aspire to less than this sort of wisdom ourselves. And who is better prepared to educate others than he who himself possesses the riches of Christian wisdom? The whole wide world is his to impart, and God is at the very heart of this world, to be known and loved.

I am sure that it is obvious to all of you how this spiritual challenge for Christian wisdom in our day affects the growth and fruitful development of Notre Dame. The vital response to this challenge can only come from all of our faculty and administration. No one is unimportant in this quest for wisdom, and in our commitment to impart wisdom to the thousands of Notre Dame students. For these young men will soon face in their own lives not only the physical challenge of achieving economic security for themselves and their families, but they will soon meet the deeper and more significant spiritual challenge of living wisely in a world given over to many forms of foolishness.

May God, the Holy Spirit, fill all of us with wisdom today and through the year, and may Notre Dame, the Mother of God and the seat of wisdom, be our beacon along the way.

1 9 5 3

A Theology of History

and Education

I, therefore, a prisoner in the Lord, beseech you that you walk worthy of the vocation in which you are called.

With all humility and mildness, with patience, supporting one another in charity.

Careful to keep the unity of the Spirit in the bond of peace.

One body and one Spirit; as you are called in one hope of your calling.

One Lord, one faith, one baptism.

One God and Father of all, who is above all, and through all, and in us all.

Ephesians: 4:1-6

THE opening of the new schoolyear provides me with the pleasant opportunity of speaking to you about the past, present, and future of the University. More effective than mere words, it gives us all the opportunity of offering the labors of the coming year to the service of God and men, in union with the greatest service of all time, the full offering of the Son of God to His Father, Calvary renewed, in the Holy Sacrifice of the Mass. This particular Mass is always the Mass of the Holy Spirit, the Spirit of Holiness and Truth, for it is under His Divine guidance and help that we work — that our days may be spent in the most efficacious kind of charity that brings men close to God in truth.

Last year, I spoke to you of Christian wisdom, the final purpose and goal of all University education, that wisdom which must characterize us as teachers and inspire our students as learners.

This year, a new page unfolds in the history of Notre Dame. Standing by itself, this could be a very trite and banal statement. But I mean to make it the topic sentence of all that will be said this morning. There are many possible attitudes that we might have at this hour. Perhaps the worst attitude would be to assume that this is just another hour, ushering in just another year in a history already one hundred and eleven years old at Notre Dame. Such an attitude is characteristic of ivy-covered minds, which unlike ivy-covered buildings, are no asset to a university. Human beings cannot long live happily, or energetically, or intelligently, or especially

13

fruitfully in an atmosphere that embalms history as mere glories of the past with no reference to the present or the future.

We have had our glorious days of the past at Notre Dame. The testimony of the past is enshrined all around us in our buildings, our monuments, our venerable traditions, and, especially, in the lives and accomplishments of our graduates. But again, history does not end until the life of man and his institutions end. What we need superlatively today is a consciousness that, through us and our lives here, the history of Notre Dame is still being written. We can be proud of past glories, but we cannot rest in them. Nor can we assume that the distinctions of the past will continue in the future without the same burning vision of divine faith and the same valiant measure of human effort that created distinction here in years past.

Many contemporary European scholars have highlighted this basic truth with reference to what might be called a Christian philosophy or theology of history. Their basic thesis agrees in this, that apart from the Judeo-Christian tradition, there can be no possible theology of history. To formulate any theology of history, one must have a sense of the purposefulness of man's life today, some sense of origin, and middle ground, and ultimate fulfillment. There must be some centrality or focus to all that happens, some inner dynamism that derives unity and meaning from a long succession of individual human acts.

Such a theology of history is not easily come by. Greek thought, that wisdom of the world to which St. Paul so often refers, found many answers to perplexing human questions, but even the Greek philosophers failed to find a meaningful direction in the unfolding of human events

and historical structures. Greek philosophy centers about
the logos, the "idea" as something fixed and eternal and
of inexorable necessity. Thus for them, time was an
eternal circle, within which nothing is new and all, of
necessity, re-occurs. Even the soul is caught up in this
necessity through the process of metempsychosis, the
transmigration of souls. Human happiness became a
vague and illusory reality attained by an escape from the
determinism and pessimism of time's eternal circle of
necessarily recurring events. Happiness in a sense involved a flight from time, leaving today, to contemplate
the eternal.

Neither has Eastern Hindu philosophy found the inner
meaning of history. Like the Greeks, their salvation too
comes by escaping the temporal reality of history, in
nirvana and reincarnation.

For these ancient wisdoms, there is little hope for
meaning and purpose in life today. It is no mere chance
that their golden ages are always in the past.

We are reminded here of a great question posed by
the recent Cardinal Archbishop of Paris: "Are we a
pawn of chance, subject to an inexorable fate at the
hands of a blind brutality of material forces? Or is there
above everything here below another power full of intelligence and love, which sees all and judges all? Is there a
Providence?"

The answer to this question is also the reason why
the Judao-Christian tradition alone gives meaning to
the history of the past, the task today, and the goal of
the future. By divine revelation in the Old and New
Testaments, God breaks into history from beyond time.
For us, time and history are linear, rather than circular.
There is a beginning of time and of man, and there is
an end towards which we are progressing through time

and history. Our God is not the faceless god of the Greek metaphysicians, nor is the human person merely a mask. Our God has entered history as the living God of prophecy and promise, and we, too, enter the drama of history as men having faith in the prophecy and freedom to follow the promise. Our history acquires purpose and meaning not only from the past in which it began, but in the present through which we traverse towards the fulfillment of the future. This is true of every man, of every nation of men, of every human institution, and it is also true of this University.

The key notion in all of this is *faith*. It is important to realize that only those religions whose revelation is inseparable from human history are based on *faith*. This faith is a faith in the word of the living God who made the world and gave it a purpose. It is also a faith in an all-powerful God who takes a part in every human event, and yet respects the freedom of human persons. Only such a living faith spells the difference between the pagan and the Christian in the face of history. For the pagan, a frustrated pessimism in the face of the inevitable. For the Christian, a bright optimism in the presence of God working through men in history. Providence, for the Christian, is one of the attributes of God. Providence implies a purpose and a fulfillment. Equally important, Providence involves a solicitous interest on the part of an omnipotent God in the efforts of a finite man to have faith in the promise and to seek the fulfillment courageously. Optimism then is indeed the order of the day, no matter what the turn of events, no matter how far we have come, no matter how far we have yet to go.

And if this optimism is born of faith in God, certainly that same faith engenders additional wellsprings of progressive human action in the supernatural virtues of hope and charity. For if faith regards the promise of God, hope looks confidently to the realization of the promise, and charity will go to work today to speed the realization of the promise accepted by faith and anticipated by hope.

There is no flight from time in all of this, for the promise was made in time and must be sought in time. And the story of the quest is the meaning of all human history.

In general, this is the thesis accepted by those who see in the Judao-Christian tradition alone, a meaning and a purpose to history.

But beyond this point, there is a basic disagreement among Christians today as to what the Christian attitude should be in the face of the historical difficulties of the purely temporal order.

The resolution of this basic difference is highly significant to the point we are attempting to make today. Karl Barth of Basel perhaps expresses best one possible Christian attitude in the face of the temporal difficulties of our times. His attitude is called the eschatological view which means simply that our supernatural vocation to share the life of God here and in eternity is of such transcendent value, that we should not concern ourselves with the comparatively ephemeral problems of human progress, science, culture, literature, or art. Temporal progress is unimportant while eternity beckons. We have here a passing city which does not merit our careful attention. While the utter secularism of our days might press us in this direction, and while the historical situation does appear to be a hopeless tangle of times, this attitude is strangely reminiscent of the Greek flight from time which is hardly acceptable or heroic in our times, even though there are bitter reasons for fleeing, and a haven of more certain hope ahead, in the Christian scheme of things.

The other attitude which I commend to you today is most compelling because of the most important fact in all human history. God became man and dwelt amongst us. History is now centered in this all important fact. All before Christ prepares for and anticipates His coming. All after Christ is the fulfillment of what He came to do. And all of us have a part in the doing, and in history, even though we are free to do our part well or poorly. Christ is the central focus and meaning of history in the Christian scheme of things.

There is no human event, no human progress in knowledge, science, or art that cannot be consecrated to a higher service, now that God has literally become man and dwelt amongst us. Historians can recognize the unique influence of the man of Galilee. Only Faith can see the utter uniqueness of God's great liturgy which is realized in Christ, in whom, and through whom, and with whom all creation is drawn to the service of God as a divine symphony in which all of us play a significant part.

Men endowed with this incarnational approach to the world today are certainly committed to human progress of all kinds. University men are even more particularly committed to take an active part in the program of creative ideas, the intellectual apostolate. We do not rest in human reason, or human values, or human science — but we certainly do begin our progress in time with all that is human in its excellence. Then, after the pattern of the Incarnation, we consecrate all our human excellence to the transforming influence of Christ in our times. Our prime concern must be to offer a worthy gift to the service of God and man. Certainly,

we should not offer as our part in this divine symphony
of all creation, the sour notes of intellectual mediocrity
or educational complacency.

This brings us back to our original theme — a statement that certainly is trite if made without reflection, and
banal if uttered without purpose: "This year, at this
hour, a new page unfolds in the history of Notre Dame."
The mere statement becomes exciting if we see ourselves
as actors rather than mere spectators of history. It becomes challenging when we realize that Notre Dame can
grow this year if all of us, Faculty, Administration, and
Students, grow in wisdom and in grace. The statement
becomes a bit frightening if you measure your own
deficiencies, as I do mine, against the promise of what
Notre Dame can be, and should be, this year and in the
years to come. Remember always that ours are deeper
and more significant goals than mere material security
and prosperity. Our aim must be a Christian humanism
born of the Incarnation of the Son of God, a humanism
embracing all the wide dimensions of the world and the
human spirit, a humanism that is adequate to the designs
of God for Notre Dame, named and consecrated as we
are to the honor of her who is most perfectly, most
beautifully, most gracefully, and most wisely human.

We do not reach these goals of the spirit by merely
balancing the budget, or maintaining a full enrollment,
or by building buildings, or winning national champion-
ships. We only reach our goal in its fullness by growing
together, in faith, and in hope, and in charity, towards
the full stature of Christian manhood, consecrated in the
growing perfection of all our human powers of mind and
will to the service of God and men, in Christ.

As this new page is unfolded, let each of us con-
sciously reach for it and think what we shall write upon

the page this year. I only ask that whatever you write be written in the spirit of faith and hope and charity, which never fails. And for all of you at this hour I would offer the prayer that all of our priests recite before examining their consciences in Corby Hall Chapel each noon:

O Jesus, living in Mary, come and live in Thy servants, in the spirit of Thy holiness, in the fullness of Thy power, in the perfection of Thy ways, in the truth of Thy virtues, in the communication of Thy mysteries. Triumph over all enemies by Thy Spirit for the glory of the Father. O Lord open the eyes and ears of my heart that I may understand Thy oracles and perform Thy Holy Will. Amen.

1 9 5 4

The Mission
of a
Catholic University

God's gift it is, if speech answers to thought of mine, and thought of mine to the message I am entrusted with. Who else can show wise men the true path, check them when they stray? We are in his hands, we and every word of ours; our prudence in act, our skill in craftsmanship. Sure knowledge he has imparted to me of all that is; how the world is ordered, what influence have the elements . . . all the mysteries and all the surprises of nature were made known to me; wisdom herself taught me, that is the designer of them all.

Nothing so agile that it can match wisdom for agility; nothing can penetrate this way and that, ethereal as she. Steam that ascends from the fervour of divine activity, pure effluence of his glory who is God all-powerful, she feels no passing taint; she, the glow that radiates from eternal light, she, the untarnished mirror of God's majesty, she, the faithful echo of his goodness. Alone, with none to aid her, she is all-powerful; herself ever unchanged, she makes all things new; age after age she finds her way into holy men's hearts, turning them into friends and spokesmen of God. Her familiars it is, none other, that God loves. Brightness is hers beyond the brightness of the sun, and all the starry host; match her with light itself, and she outvies it; light must still alternate with darkness, but where is the conspiracy can pull down wisdom from her throne?

Wisdom: 7:15-30

W E BEGIN the school year today, as a faculty and student body, in prayer. I have mentioned at the opening Mass in other years that we offer this Mass to God, the Holy Spirit, that we might, as a faculty and student body, be granted two great graces: Wisdom to see the road ahead this year in light of the needs of time and eternity; and, secondly, the courage to do all that each of us must do to make our personal contribution to the living, growing reality of Notre Dame.

Others might well be here in our place today. There are other men, more intelligent, more courageous than we are, more zealous men, holier men. But, by the grace of God, we are what we are. And, in the Providence of God, we are Notre Dame this year. So being what we are, no more and no less, we pray for light to see and strength to do. To see what, then, and to do what?

I fear at times that all of us are too close to what is happening here to grasp the real vision of what we are trying to do, even to appreciate what we are praying for today. We are not alone in this. Hundreds of universities are beginning a new school year this month. Many of them are larger than Notre Dame, some of them are older. But the only significant question today is: How many of them are better than Notre Dame as universities. Excellence as such has no direct relation to size or age. A small diamond is better than a huge rhinestone, and a youthful saint is better than an aged sinner. Excellence in the case of universities, however, does have a direct relation to what universities are supposed to do and how they are performing their proper function. It is highly significant to ask in this context: How do we compare?

Comparisons are said to be odious. I suspect that this dictum was coined by those who compared poorly with the best of their kind. The comparison in this present instance is particularly complicated by the general confusion regarding the *purpose* of university education: the only valid standard by which university excellence may be judged. Before we compare ourselves with any others, we should at least be clear ourselves as to what we are aspiring to do, and the adequacy of our means. Someone might say at this juncture: Is it not slightly ridiculous, after 112 years of operation, to ask what are we trying to do? If you think it ridiculous try to answer the question yourself, in a way that will do justice to the history and the tradition of the highest Catholic learning.

We have grown greatly in the past 112 years. We have our own power plant, fire station, laundry, hotel, and will shortly have our own shopping center and television station. However related these are to the general operation here, it would be ridiculous to see in them, or even in our magnificent academic buildings, an indication of excellence in our primary objective as a great Catholic university. In any consideration of physical plant, we compare favorably with many of the best universities, but ultimately the physical comparison is fruitless and somewhat unrelated to excellence as a university. The inner burning question is still pressing for an answer. What are we primarily trying to do and how are we doing it?

The question might be rephrased and asked in more familiar form: Why have a great Catholic university, or any Catholic university at all? The only legitimate answer would have to demonstrate that a Catholic university has a function, as university and precisely as Catholic, ful-

filled by no other. This function would have to meet a
real and vital need in the world today, a need being met
by no other agent. All other universities would suffer by
comparison to such a providential institution. This institution would be proud of its place in the world, would
fulfill its mission with enthusiastic zeal and unrelenting
effort.

We are praying this morning in the Mass for the wisdom and the courage to be such an institution, to be not
just what we are today and have been, however good
that is, but to be what, by the Grace of God and the
demand of the times, and the richness of our heritage,
Notre Dame could and should be.

Universities, like all other human institutions, came
into being because men saw in them an answer to an
urgent human need. Of course, these needs vary somewhat from age to age. This shifting of priorities, of prime
urgencies, results in a varied emphasis on the part of the
university. This much though, I think, should be stated
as a matter of stable principle regarding university objectives, irrespective of the actual cultural, political,
religious, or economic climate of any age: The university is by its essential nature committed to the mission of
learning and teaching. The university is born when
human minds are at work together for intellectual purposes. The university prospers when men are willing to
stand firmly for the value of things intellectual, to devote
themselves wholeheartedly to study and learning and
teaching that the human intellect may "become richer
and stronger, broader in appreciation and sympathy,
more firm in judgement, more sure in action . . . to gain
at last some measure of wisdom, some vision of truth,
some understanding of the Will of God."

It was such a vision and such an intellectual human

need that first drew men together in an association that became a university at Paris, Bologna, Louvain, Chartres, Oxford, and Cambridge. It might be noted that all these were Catholic universities too, since all their learning was ordered under the egis of theology, the highest wisdom. They were not called Catholic then, as there was nothing else comparable that would necessitate this qualification. They are not Catholic today because much has happened since, religiously, culturally, politically, and economically, to further complicate this essential intellectual task of the university. There is nothing we can do to change what has transpired since the founding of the first universities. But we can and must try to understand this historical background in its dynamism and general direction, because it has fashioned the world we live in today. Our particular task as a modern Catholic university is certainly more complicated than in mediaeval times. Yet, our work today is more challenging, and certainly more vitally needed because of the climate in which we do live.

How summarize what has happened? The very listing of the historical figures brings to mind the strong currents of new theologies and new philosophies that made the ordered flow of knowledge a swirling, churning vortex of conflicting assertions and denials. Luther and Calvin, Francis Bacon, Descartes, and Rousseau, Hobbes, Locke, and Voltaire, Hume, Kant, and Hegel, Darwin, James, and Dewey. This is part of the geneology.

It is equally difficult to summarize the kaleidoscopic nightmare of isms that have ebbed and flowed through these past four centuries; rationalism, skepticism, agnosticism and atheism; voluntarism, pragmatism, dialectic materialism, and existentialism; positivism, scientism, mechanism, and relativism. However good the intentions, however valid the critical spirit, however sincere the authors, one cannot view the actual results — the world we have inherited today — without shuddering at the formidable task of putting all the pieces back into order again. Nothing has escaped this intellectual disorder — neither man in his spirit, his mind and his will, not society, government, history, or law, not the world itself, nor God who made it. All are denied, denatured, despiritualized. And as a somber closing note, we find a growing distrust of intellectuals and things intellectual by those who should ordinarily look to great minds for leadership.

One ray of light, one road of hope remains. Minds have created this disorder and minds alone can begin to remake the order that has largely been lost. It was for this purpose that God gave us our minds — that there might be order and ordered growth in man and in his world. It was for this purpose that the mediaeval universities were founded — to further the acquisition of those intellectual virtues of understanding, wisdom, science, prudence, and art. It was through such discipline of the mind that the first universities hoped to influence persons and society, to quench the thirst for truth in the minds of men, to enable the intelligence of man to order and dispose human acts in the light of truth in all its fullness. This was a high calling at that time. It is an even higher calling today, given the need of our times for what we alone as a Catholic University can offer: adequacy of knowledge, truth in all its fullness, human and divine.

A Protestant educator had to remind us recently that ours is the richest and most constant intellectual tradition in the Western World. What does this tradition say? It says that there is a God, Father, Son and Holy Spirit.

That He made all that is, and man particularly after His
image and likeness: with spiritual endowments of intelligence and free will, and an eternal destiny of perfect
happiness with God. It says that man is fallen, but not
totally corrupted, that Adam's fall was a kind of felic-
itous error since the Son of God became man in the person of Jesus Christ. That Christ lived and died to redeem
us, and founded an age-long mystical body to continue
His work of incarnation and redemption, to teach,
govern, and sanctify all men in Christ. That men are
persons, free and equal as sons of God and brothers of
Christ, endowed with dignity and called to greatness.
This tradition prizes the power of man's mind in all of
its search for truth and the expression of truth through
science, art, philosophy, and, most highly, through
theology, wherein man is given a direct assist in his
quest for truth through God's own revelation. This tradition prizes the freedom of man, not as absolute, but
as a power to choose what is best, even the divine. This
tradition cherishes and promotes the inviolability of
man's rights as a person, seeks justice and charity, law
and order, truth, the good and the beautiful. The cen-
turies-long tradition of Christian wisdom seeks all of these
things in order and symmetry, in peace and understanding, and would have them produce a profound and rich
Christian culture today, even as in the latter dark ages it
disciplined minds and souls and drew men from barbarism into a world of natural and supernatural reality.
This tradition is the same one that created legal institutions when the Western World was in transition from
barbarism to civilization; this tradition fostered the arts,
preserved the documents, founded the schools and universities and taught men that they could know, love, and
serve God while transfiguring the natural world by the

intelligence, and freedom, and creativity that are in man's nature because he is made in God's image.

If we have been at times unmindful of this tradition, how could we have forgotten the great persons who made it live and grow in their day? Athanasius, Leo, Augustine, Ambrose, Gregory, Bede, Bernard, Albert, Aquinas, Bonaventure, all intellectual giants, and holy men, too, for as Rabanus Maurus said, no one can perfectly achieve wisdom unless he loves God. Then there were the great creative geniuses in literature and the arts — Dante, Chaucer, Fra Angelico, Michelangelo, Da Vinci, Thomas More, Palestrina, Pascal; science has had its share and more — Copernicus, Galileo, Linacre, Lavoisier, Pasteur, Mendel, our own Nieuwland.

How, one might ask, could the intellectual climate of the Western World have become so clouded if such is the strong tradition and such the valiant men. Perhaps the answer to this question may hurt, but it should be faced. The tradition of Christian wisdom was more vital centuries ago than it is today. The great Catholic scholars were more plentiful in the past than they are in the present. Why? I fear that the dynamic and creative forces behind the movement were dissipated by the turn of events and became less vital. Christian philosophy spent itself in dialectics and sterile distinctions, did not keep pace with an awakening scientific curiosity and method. Catholic theology repeated itself into formalistic patterns that were more mindful of the enemy without than the eternal spring of new Christian life and wisdom within. We defended the walls, but we ceased to build the city, and we looked too seldom to the new problems beyond the walls in the new secularistic city of man.

All this may be explained away by saying that at least we still live and still do have schools and universities —

but again comes the agonizing inquiry: Are we really
doing all we might do to redeem and re-order and revivify
the world in which we live today?

I grant that it is easy to condemn the past. Our own
American past gives us much to be thankful for. Notre
Dame's own history is a thrilling account of sacrifice,
devotion, and sheer pioneering doggedness that brought
this University from a low grade grammar school to what
it is today.

But the present and the future are our immediate problem as we begin the 113th year in Notre Dame's history.
I would say to you today that the pioneering days of
childhood and youth are over. And if we are staggered
to think of the Herculean tasks already performed in
childhood and youth, I would further stagger you with
the thought that to be true to our vital mission, even
more prodigious tasks are ahead to achieve maturity.

I would apply to ourselves today the fullness of the
words of two great men, Leo XIII and Bishop Spaulding
regarding universities:

Leo XIII wrote: "The end of the Catholic university
forever will be this: with the light of Catholic truth show-
ing the way to provide for youth in our country the *fullness* and the *best* of learning on the highest levels."

And Bishop Spaulding: "A true university will be the
home of ancient wisdom and new learning; it will teach
the best that is known and encourage research; it will
stimulate thought, refine taste, and awaken a love of
excellence; it will be at once a scientific institute, a school
of culture and a training ground in the business of life;
it will educate the minds that give direction to the age,
it will be the nursery of ideas, a center of influence . . .
that which is the strongest in man is mind, and when a

mind truly vigorous, open, supple and illuminated reveals itself, we follow in its path of light."

Here is no longer a mere physical task of survival in a raw new land. Here is a demanding spiritual task of the highest order, in fullest accord with the rich age-old tradition of Christian wisdom. Here is an apostolate that no secular university today can undertake — for they are largely cut off from the tradition of adequate knowledge which comes only through faith in the mind and faith in God, the highest wisdom of Christian philosophy and Catholic theology.

Here is a task that requires that we be conscious of our past heritage, and enthusiastic in bringing new insights of Christian wisdom to the present. Here is a task for the greatest minds, and the most devoted hearts and completely dedicated lives.

I know of no other spot on earth where we might make a better beginning than here at Notre Dame, where we might inaugurate a new center of Christian culture to effect a re-awakening of the potential of Christian wisdom applied to the problems of our age.

This is no work of defense, no declaration of war, no practice in isolation, but a move to revitalize our own understanding of the treasure of supreme intellectualism and divine faith, wedded in strength and beauty. It means working together, each with our own particular talents to exploit the full power of Christian wisdom to order what is disordered, to complete what is good but incomplete, to meet insufficient knowledge with the fullness of truth, to give a new direction and a wider, saner perspective to all that is good and true in our times.

The time is ripe, The old errors are sunk in frustration, and pessimism and disorder. Men of good will are not wanting. Darkness awaits a light. We have done and are doing, a wide variety of good things at Notre Dame. If we do everything else and fail in this, our proper task, our high calling, our providential mission, then as we pray in the presence of God here today, we will be unworthy servants, and a failure as a Catholic university.

Let us pray then, sincerely and humbly this morning, as we begin another academic year. Let us ask again and again for wisdom and courage, the light to see and the strength to do what the times demand and the richness of our heritage promises.

1 9 5 5

Education

in a World

of Social Challenge

If you continue in my word, you shall be my disciples indeed.
And you shall know the truth, and the truth shall make you free.

John: 8:31-32

A T THE beginning of each school year, we pause for a solemn moment of prayer: that God may bless our mutual endeavor of the months to come, and that He may also confirm each of us in our dedication to this lofty endeavor that demands the best that is in each of us.

We also pause for a few moments this morning to consider some aspect of the work at hand, to glean, if possible, some added inspiration from the thought that ours is no trivial task, no ordinary calling.

This year, I shall try to review what might be termed the social challenge of the educative process. Social development is not the primary purpose of education, but neither is it an unimportant by-product. Education is primarily concerned with an individual person. We attempt as teachers to draw to some fulfillment the inner powers of the person: his capacity for discerning truth, his yearning for the inner freedom which is nurtured by the growing possession of truth, integrated knowledge and ultimately wisdom which gives meaning and conscious order to all that is known. Education must also, and more indirectly, be a school of love, for truth and beauty and the good things of life are not merely to be known, but to be assimilated in the person who is made to possess by love as well as to see by knowledge.

Education and the work of educators could cease at this point, if the person educated could live his life in solitary contemplation and love. But the student, like ourselves, is living in an historic moment of time, in a real world with all its actual tensions and current crises.

35

The university cannot abstract itself or its students from the realities of past history or the anguish of the present crisis. Even if the university accomplishes its primary mission in relative seclusion from the intemperate cross currents of the forum and the market place, it cannot shelter itself or its students from the conflict of ideas that is the most real substratum of these cross currents.

Ideas are engaged today in mortal conflict, and at the center of the struggle is the soul of man, his dignity, the truth by which alone he can live, his freedom to be what he was created to be. This man, whose soul and dignity and freedom are at stake, is the same man who is being educated. If in the process, he is not equipped to recognize the conflict of his times, to discern its basic issues, and to accept what part he must play to aid in final victory, then the university is indeed a parasite in a society that looks to it for leadership, and knowledge, for wisdom and integrity, at least in the minds and hearts of its graduates.

The first pages of recorded human history tell the story of conflict: good against evil, truth against falsehood, order against anarchy, obedience against pride, spirit against matter. It was not a story of victory then, nor is it a story of victory today in the world-wide present version of the original episode in the Garden of Eden. There have been classical victories and classical defeats in the age-old struggle, and the battle lines have been extended and complicated in the intervening centuries.

What perhaps somewhat simplifies the picture today is that at least in the realm of basic ideology the battle line is clearly drawn. We can speak of the free world where the dominant social structures try to respect what is most sacred in Western Culture: the dignity of man, his basic rights and freedoms, his inner aspirations for what is called the pursuit of happiness: the good life in a good society. And we can speak of the other half of the world, where this concept of man does not obtain and is not respected.

Between these two worlds there is, and must be, real conflict. The terms of the conflict may change from year to year: now cold war, now lukewarm war, now again war disguised as peaceful co-existence. Yet, whatever the actual terms of the conflict, conflict it is, and conflict it will be as long as the soul of man is at stake, and the power of evil is at large.

There are many illusory solutions offered to end the present conflict: diplomatic moves and counter moves, the implied threat of more numerous and more destructive nuclear weapons, the full-fledged chicanery of every means of modern propaganda to strengthen one's position and to weaken that of the enemy. These and other solutions are illusory, because they fail to recognize that the conflict is not basically military, political, or economic. At heart, the conflict is both philosophical and theological. The actual battlefield is in the realm of ideas. No matter what the physical or material forces involved, ultimately it is ideas that will prevail, truth that will gain or lose in this struggle for the souls of men.

How does all of this affect the university and its mission of educating students in this year which we officially begin today? Obviously, we must have true and good ideas ourselves if we are to teach our students with conviction and inspire them to hunger, to search for, to find and to embrace the truth. For it is only the truth ultimately that will make us truly free.

How is the truth represented today on our side of the crucial struggle? We are oratorically so often critical of the opposition that the obvious assumption is that he is

all wrong and that we are all right. But in a more reflective mood, might we not ask how right we really are,
or to put it another way, if we are right, are we right for
the right reasons. Our assessment of this situation will
affect mightily the attitudes that are reflected in our
educational process.

No one in the West would seriously question the fundamental truth of the democratic charter. But too few
of us question the present day vitality of its tap-roots:
the soul of Christianity and Western culture from which
it laboriously grew. The opposition at least is clear about
its precedents: Communism is the product of naturalism
and materialism full blown. The Communist clearly recognizes totalitarianism as an end in itself to be furthered
by any means. Perhaps because of its more recent origin,
the Communist sees more clearly the logical and vital
connection between his philosophy and its conclusions in
the practical order of social life.

But how many in the West would recognize that
democracy, unlike the totalitarian scheme, is not an end
in itself — but a temporal means of preserving the ultimate human values of a spiritual order: the dignity of
man, his rights and responsibilities to his fellow men
under God, man's inner spiritual freedom to seek a
personal destiny that transcends temporal society. These
spiritual values can be achieved by means of a democratic
society. They may also exist, to some extent, without the
precise political order that we have, but democracy, as
we know it, cannot exist without these spiritual values.
The inner contradiction of our day is simply this: that
we have accepted the democratic charter, enjoyed a great
and wonderful gift of ages past, a gift flowing from the
inner dynamism of Christianity and from a deep dedication to the value of the spirit in man, and then, having

accepted the fruit, we have forgotten the root and branch. We have, in large measure in the West, allowed the soul of our culture to die, while living on the rich, but rapidly diminishing, heritage of the past.

This is what Plato long ago condemned as "living by habit without fixed principle." Ours is the house now resting on sand about which Our Lord warned us. The fair day has passed, the winds and the rains are come. We must now look to the foundations of our social order. It is no longer reasonable or honest enough to accept conclusions and to abdicate the principles which alone can validate the conclusions.

How popular, or even acceptable, in present day university circles are the vital philosophical principles, the living Christian faith that gave birth to the democratic charter after ages of tyranny and human oppression? Most universities teach everything but theology, the science of faith. The philosophy in vogue today is strangely akin to that naturalism and materialism that the opposition so logically pursues.

Glance for a moment at these philosophies. Naturalism denies outright man's relation both to an ultimate order of values and to God who is the source of these absolutes. Naturalism thus divorces man from the spiritual and moral order to which he belongs and without which he will be destitute of any reasonable order or direction in life. Standing all alone, endowed with perfectibility by courtesy of Rousseau, man is left without any norm or sanction beyond himself and his own desires, individual when he can press them, and collective when they are pressed upon him. The natural result is pride and egotism. All man has left to worship or serve is himself or his false gods of money, power, nation or race.

At this point, try to see the logic of those educators in our day who in practice try to preserve the dignity of man while intellectually subscribing to a basically materialistic philosophy that recognizes man as little more than a highly developed animal. And where is the logic of still enjoying a democratic charter, derived from belief in absolute spiritual and moral values, long after these same basic values have been discarded from the educational process as unsophisticated, or archaic, or what is most devastating today, unscientific.

We might have lingered longer in this sorry state of intellectual schizophrenia had not the present crisis developed. Perhaps in the Providence of God, Communism will do this service to the world, and especially to us of the Western World, to demonstrate in its starkest reality the logical consequences in the social order of a fully conscious naturalistic and materialistic concept of man and his destiny.

We are concerned no longer in the West with a more or less perfect democratic charter, but with the life or death of this idea and its reality in the face of a fiercely competitive idea and reality that will have all the world or nothing. This is no high-school debate, but a life and death struggle with naturalism and materialism on the march, inflamed with pride and passion and zeal, armed with an apocalyptic drive, vast political power, clever propaganda, and the vision of world domination.

Against this force shall we oppose a democratic charter that is unsure of its presuppositions, robbed of the strength it once drew from vital dynamic principles? Shall we dare to hope for victory if we have thrown away our arms — the sword of the spirit, the might of the Lord of Hosts, the force of vital ideas, the courageous traditions of men who believed, and hoped and loved —

that truth might prevail and that man, under God, might be truly free to live his life and to achieve his destiny in a social order based on absolute justice and law?

The basic social problem of the West would still be with us tomorrow if Communism were obliterated today. Without the pressure of Communism, we would not be more strong, only less harassed. The inner dynamism of the democratic charter would still need strengthening to survive, even if it were alone in this world. Death comes to a culture or a civilization, not solely from external pressures, but, even more often, from the inner withering of a vital principle, from a loss of faith, from moral anemia, and from the abdication of a basic commitment to truth and integrity. Yes, even without the threat of Communism, we would still be obliged to revitalize our faith, to revivify basic respect for our philosophical roots, not because they are useful or helpful to us in this conflict, but because they are true.

Here then, in the realm of truth, is the mission of the university manifest. If our graduates are to have a vital part in the struggle for men's souls, they must begin by achieving true wisdom and freedom in their own souls. This inner development may seem distant from the dramatic issues of Washington, Moscow, and Geneva. But the action that takes place in those distant scenes is the result of ideas that began their existence in the minds of men like Machiavelli, Kant, Rousseau, Hegel, Hobbes, Marx, Engels, Lenin, and Stalin on the one hand, and, on the other, ideas that burgeoned in the minds of Plato and Aristotle, Augustine and Aquinas, Madison and Jefferson, Washington and Lincoln. Throughout the ideas of the latter, there is ever present the leaven of the divine ideas of Christ, and the accumulated wisdom of Western concern for the dignity of

man, his inalienable rights, his responsibilities to God
and his fellow men, justice, law, and equity.

A University today will have an impact on the progress of man and human society in direct proportion to
the truth of the heritage it imparts to its students.

I would only like to signalize today two of these basic
truths that highlight the current conflict of ideas in the
social order. They are likewise truths that traditionally
have formed the cornerstone at Notre Dame, for an
education productive of responsible leadership in the
social order.

The first and most fundamental truth is the existence
of one supreme, personal God, above and beyond history,
infinite in knowledge and power, the Creator and Pre-
server of all that is, the Reality upon Whom all creation,
including man, depends, the beginning and the end. One
God in Three Divine Persons, Father of Whom we are
called to be sons, Son Incarnate of Whom we are brothers, Holy Spirit, the source of our highest inspiration for
truth and love.

The antithesis of this idea is atheism — the cornerstone of the opposition, the one basic reason that Communism is evil. No God, no creation, no providence, no
spiritual reality, no freedom for good or evil, no ultimate
beyond time, no higher norm for law, no eternal sanction for justice, no real basis for charity, no glimmer of
immortality, no rights that are inalienable, no dedication
that is divine, no order beyond nature, no meaning beyond matter.

Here is opposition of ideas that brooks no compromise.
You are either for God or against Him; He is the center
of human life or man is his own center. If God has
spoken, if He has established an economy of salvation,
then this is the all important truth. Man can deny reality,

truth, the good — but then he must create his own substitutes for these realities. And he must live with his petty substitutes — until ultimately reality, truth, and the good will emerge to answer the anguished cry of a miserable humanity that pays the awful price of its denial.

Secondly, there is the truth of man, made in the image and likeness of God, made to glory in truth, made to love what is good and to enjoy beauty. Not the self-sufficient man of the naturalists, not the earthbound man of the materialists, but man who possesses dignity and immortality as a son of God and a brother of Christ, man with all the inalienable rights he needs to act humanly, man fallen and yet redeemed, man endowed with divine life in his spirit through the grace of Christ, man who is a microcosm of the whole created universe, man whose spirit is free to range the universe, to love God and all else in God, man who shares the passion of Christ and the triumph of the Risen Christ.

And then there is the man of the Communists: akin only to the animals in his body, slave of the state, knowing only what can be seen and felt and sensed, determined by blind economic force, made to believe that anarchy is order, force is freedom, error is truth and slavery is liberation. Man with no hope beyond bread and the reign of the proletariat under the Commissars, man not a little less than the angels, but just a little above the beasts.

Here again is an uncompromising conflict of ideas. We are either on one side, or on the other. Armies may wage war, diplomats may parley, boundaries may be shifted, but in the end it is the idea that will win or lose. And it is only the truth that will set man free.

We might have lived in a different age, or not at all. We might have engaged ourselves in work of less significance or importance than education. But in the Providence of God, we live today. We are engaged in this work, and the only important question to ask ourselves is this: are we equal to the historical moment we face? Can we find within ourselves that burning commitment to the truth of God and His revelation, that consecration to the truth of man as we know him? And can we engender in a new generation of students a love of these basic truths, a commitment to what is good for man in the sight of God, a generosity to serve God and men for a resolution of the present conflict in modern society? We do not pray today that somehow all crises will miraculously cease, for crisis is the pattern of history and always will be. We only ask, humbly and confidently, that we may be worthy of the truth that is ours, for those on the side of truth are on the side of God, and, eventually on the side of ultimate victory. May Mary, Seat of Wisdom, guide us on our way this year.

1 9 5 6

The Divine Element

in Education

And He (Christ) himself gave some men as apostles, and some as prophets, others again as evangelists, and others as pastors and teachers, in order to perfect the saints for a work of ministry, for building up the body of Christ, until we all attain to the unity of the faith, and of the deep knowledge of the Son of God, to perfect manhood, to the mature measure of the fullness of Christ.

Ephesians: 4:11-13

THIS morning, as we begin a new school year with the Solemn Mass of the Holy Spirit, I would like to ponder with you some of the implications of the inspired words of St. Paul which we have just read. Last week, I was speaking with an alumnus who had not been on this campus for twenty years. He was, of course, astounded at the growth that is everywhere manifest. For those of us who live and work here, the blessings of the past twenty years are indeed a cause for joy and real reason for thanksgiving.

I know you will forgive me if I pause in this feeling of satisfaction, and ask some disturbing questions. In many ways, the growth and progress of Notre Dame have paralleled the magnificent advance of our own beloved America. Most human institutions, even of religious origin, tend to mirror in many ways the circumstantial aspects of the times, the spirit, yes, even the weaknesses of the particular environment in which they grow.

Few can question the material growth of America or of Notre Dame. But the physical growth of a person or of a human institution is no guarantee of inner human growth, of mature spiritual perfection, of the kind of fulfillment that alone is important in assessing the true value of a country, a person, or an institution. Physical growth can indeed become a kind of seduction, wherein we assume, from outward appearance, the existence of inner vitality and equal accomplishment in the line of mature interior excellence.

As you know, however, the two perfections, physical and spiritual, do not necessarily go together. Nor are they achieved by the same effort, or the same means. Physical growth in an institution is mainly a matter of money, masonry, and mortar. Spiritual perfection in its essence needs none of these. Rather, it begins with the human understanding of an ideal, the consecration of human minds and hearts to a task most worthy of man, but also most difficult, because each newly conquered peak of perfection presents a newer and higher prominence behind it, yet to be climbed. It is much easier to achieve physical growth, as a person or as an institution, and then to call it a day. But this mediocre satisfaction never makes for a great person, or a great institution, because spirit alone vivifies matter and endows it with higher dignity and value.

Some thoughtful people have questioned whether or not the physical growth of America today has been matched by a corresponding development of our spiritual wisdom and moral character. The same question might be asked of Notre Dame, not in a carping spirit of criticism, but in a reflective mood of self-analysis linked to the sincere desire for the greatest possible perfection in the high task committed to us. It is certainly no less true of universities, than of men, that the unexamined life is not worth living.

The inner growth of a university depends in large measure upon the excellence of its faculty. This is much more, however, than the sum total of their individual talents, because a university is a community of scholars working together, not a mere collection of individually good minds, haphazardly and geographically assembled in one place. Now collaborative human effort in a university requires some unity of spirit and ideal, some human understanding and sharing of the great dignity of the endeavor. In the nature of the world we live in, 'with its often superficial judgments and attitudes, some members of the university community will often receive a larger measure of praise and plaudits for accomplishments that are, in reality, the work of all. Yet, at the heart of the endeavor and in the eyes of God, each member must know that he belongs and is important and vital to the task.

Our opening text from St. Paul addresses itself to this problem, in the exact context of the Church. This is helpful to us too, because Notre Dame is, among other things, a work of the Church and, moreover, the work of Notre Dame highlights one of the great opportunities and deep problems of the Church today: that of priests and laymen working fruitfully together in a common endeavor. There is a meaningful historical and theological background to the position of the laity in the Catholic Church. In modern times, some have claimed that Catholic laymen are no more than passive and silent bystanders in the work of the Church. There may be some truth in this assertion, and if there is, I do not mean to imply that inactivity, or passivity, is invariably the layman's fault, or his proper role.

As usual, history gives us an understandable background of the situation. In earliest times, St. Paul spoke with great affection of those laymen who helped him with his great mission to the gentiles. The situation of a too passive laity in recent centuries is perhaps best explained by the doctrinal emphasis on hierarchical authority following the negation of this authority in the Reformation, when the preacher was substituted for the priest, when the sermon replaced the Holy Sacrifice, and private interpretation was judged superior to traditional pronouncement. Re-emphasis in time of crisis may then have strengthened the position of embattled clergy, but quite another phenomenon is taking place today, and this time it is the laity whose position in the Church is being reaffirmed, again historically in the face of crisis. The crisis of our times is the almost universal divorce of the spiritual from the temporal order. The capital sin of our age is the process of secularism, which someone has aptly described as the practice of the absence of God. In this present crisis, the layman is the key man. The solution to the problem of secularism must be a work of mediation between the two orders which secularism separates. The layman is in a perfect position to mediate: as a member of the Church, he is in the spiritual order; and as a layman, he is, by definition, in the temporal order. However, one does not mediate merely by being in a circumstantial position to do so. The layman must understand his position, the true inner nature of the problem, and have the power to act. This is where we leave history and enter theology.

To understand fully the position of the layman in the Church, one must understand the Church. And to understand the Church, one must understand Christ. It would be utter presumption to cover this vast field of theology in so few words, but the main lines of thought may be indicated with the hope that all of you may study the matter as deeply as it deserves, and indeed requires, for full comprehension.

In the fullness of time, God sent His only begotten Son into the world to restore to men full access to eternal union with Him, to which all mankind is destined by the great goodness of God, our Creator. The work of reuniting God and man was also a task of mediation, and Christ, Our Lord, is the great, and in a true sense, the only eternal Mediator of all time. Others can only participate in His work. His basic work of mediation was accomplished for all time in His Person, by His Incarnation, wherein the Eternal Son of God is born of the Blessed Virgin Mary; God becomes man and dwells among us. God and man are substantially united in His Person. The act of sacrificial redemption on Calvary is not the end of the story, but only the beginning of the great drama of redemption and salvation that goes on as long as there are men to be saved. The important part of the story for us this morning is that while Christ's work of redemption and salvation happened once for all; yet in His divine plan it is applied, man by man, in every age, and every man has his own proper part to play in the redemptive process. It might have been different, but the fact is that Christ wished to associate us with Him, and, for this reason, He established His Church, His mystical body of which He is the Head and we the members. Christ, Our Lord, said that He came to give life and give it more abundantly. The Church is not just a juridical organization, but a lifegiving body. We are incorporated into this body by Baptism, reborn to the very divine life of Christ, Our Head. Through the sacraments, this life is nurtured and grows. We are not independent of each other: we share the same divine life, that of Christ, Our Head. In serving others, we serve Christ, and if we should despise another, we despise Christ.

The particular point I would highlight here is that no one is unimportant in the Church, because all of us have the same basic dignity as members of Christ, partakers of His divine life. All truth, all grace, all power, all dignity in the Church, from Pope to peasant, is from Christ. And because we share His life, we also share

His work of redemption, not all in the same measure, but all truly participate if the redemptive work is to be accomplished as He wishes. This is why the Catholic laity have been exhorted by every recent Holy Father to take active part in the prayer life of the Church through the liturgical movement, that together all of us may grow inwardly to the full maturity of the life of Christ. And because life is manifested by works, there has been a constant appeal for lay participation in the works of the Church through the lay apostolate. In speaking to some pilgrims at Rome, Pius XII recently said: "You do not merely belong to the Church; you are the Church." For the Church, ultimately, is the presence of Christ in the world today, in each of us, still living and working at the age-long task of bringing God to men and men to God, through Christ and in Christ. And so it may truly be concluded that, to the extent that Christ lives in us, to that extent is our work Christ-like and of eternal value.

Against this historical and theological background, I would now like to sketch briefly the task of the layman who lives in the temporal as well as the spiritual order. The great danger is twofold: that the orders be kept absolutely separate, the secularistic scheme of things, or that they be hopelessly confused, as those do who would substitute piety in one order for competence in the other. The temporal and spiritual orders are indeed distinct, but certainly need not be separate. Human nature and divine nature are distinct realities in Christ, but united in His person. His humanity did not suffer from the union, but was ineffably glorified and enriched. Nor was His divinity diminished, for only by becoming man could Christ give us the supreme evidence of God's love for man by dying for us as a man. Our work, in a modern secularistic world, must be patterned on these great supernatural realities. The layman must have a clear view of both orders if he is to be a Christian humanist in the modern world. The alternative is utter naturalism, or a pseudosupernaturalism. The layman must respect the values of both orders, too, as well as the proper objectives and techniques of both orders, if his life and work are to have balance and full significance, and if he himself is to be equal to the challenge of secularism.

In the spiritual order, the plane of the Church, the layman's action is directed towards eternal values, towards God and the things of God, towards the goal of eternal life for himself and those about him. Here the layman is engaged in liturgical and apostolic life as a member of the Body of Christ; he offers prayers and sacrifices and indeed participates in the re-offering of the Sacrifice of Christ in the Mass. He practices virtue so that Christ may be manifest in him; he lives his faith and serves with the freedom of the sons of God. This you may say is his life in Christ and God.

In the temporal order, the plane of the world, if you will, the layman's action is directed towards the good things of time. Here the layman acts as a citizen of the earthly city and he takes his legitimate part in the affairs of humanity in time. The values he works for may be of the intellectual or moral order, they will certainly involve civilization and culture, the works of science or art, the political, economic, and social exigencies of daily living. I would underscore here again that all these are real values. The important work of mediation is this: these earthly values, insofar as they are true and good, may be revivified, elevated, offered to God by the man of the spirit who engages in them. In this way, our activities in the affairs of time will never become final ends. And, on the other hand, we will not be tempted to offer to God a mediocre service in the temporal order, for God is not honored by poor art, shoddy science, shady politics, or a sensualist culture.

What is needed so desperately today is what Maritain calls the integral humanist, the whole man who is really at home, temporarily in time and eternally in eternity, the man who respects both orders, and neglects neither, the man who has been completely revivified by the grace of Christ, whose faith and hope and charity are able to renew, direct, and revivify the things of time, and to achieve the human good in all its fullness in time while ultimately referring it to the eternal good that awaits beyond. This is the man who cherishes the higher wisdom and is not afraid to let it shine through his life and work. Without this man, I know not how the elevating and eternal spirit of the Gospel, the saving presence of Christ, is going to be manifest in the many quarters of this modern world where the temporal order and the things of time have become ends in themselves, divorced from any higher wisdom, any nobler law, any breath of God and the things of God.

The world is poorer today for secularism, and will be poorer still if the work of incarnation does not take root in the lives of our laymen. I know of no place where this new breath of divine life could more effectively grow and multiply than here at Notre Dame. Many of our concerns are of the temporal order, but all about us there are reminders that this is not a lasting city. Our work of education is in the world, but never completely of the world. We have priests and laymen side by side; we are committed to a higher wisdom while working effectively for all the perfection that is possible in the things of time. And there is an undefinable spirit of devotion and consecration here that alone can explain what has already been accomplished and the great things that we yet aspire to accomplish.

We began by reading the words of St. Paul to the Ephesians, where he describes how Christ has provided for many functions in His Mystical Body, the Church, and how all of these various functions are for the building up of the Body, until we all attain to the unity of the faith, and of the deep knowledge of the Son of God, to perfect manhood, to the mature measure of the fullness of Christ. I would like to conclude with the words of St. Paul which immediately follow this passage:

We are no longer to be children, no longer to be like storm-tossed sailors, driven before the wind of each new doctrine that human subtlety, human skill in fabricating lies, may propound. We are to follow the truth, in a spirit of love, and so grow up, in everything, into a due proportion with Christ, who is our head. On him all the body depends; it is organized and unified by each contact with the source which supplies it; and thus, each limb receiving the active power it needs, it achieves its natural growth, building itself up through love.

1 9 5 7

Education in

a World

of Science

At present, we are looking at a confused reflection in a mirror; then we shall see face to face; now, I have only glimpses of knowledge; then, I shall recognize God as He has recognized me.

I Corinthians 13:12

As each new schoolyear begins, it is my duty and my honor to appear before you and to highlight some of the things we pray for in this inaugural Mass of the Holy Spirit. If one would seek a common theme in my sermons of other years, it would be this: that we are committed here at Notre Dame to a common task of uncommon importance; that this task must somehow be doubly related, first, to the modern world in which we live, with all its tensions, its agonies, its new developments, and its vivid opportunities. Our task must likewise be related to that ancient wisdom which is ours to transmit, not by blind indoctrination, but with a vital sense of its relevance to the burning questions of our age. I have never said that ours is an easy task, and have indeed underlined some of the difficulties that complicate our activities. You will recall some of these: the explosive growth of knowledge that allows real competence in one field often at the expense of overall, integrated knowledge; then there is the intellectual atmosphere of secularism, an historical reality that has resulted in a general disdain for theology and philosophy while seemingly more exciting windows of knowledge were and are being opened in other directions; then there has been our oftentimes poor and unenthusiastic comprehension of our own rich heritage, the bright light hidden under the bushel basket, the dull repetition of formulae and the all too frequent lack of burning dedication, enlightened curiosity, and hard unrelenting mental labor that alone can continue the ancient and worthy tradition of Catholic scholarship.

The particular problem that I wish to discuss with you this year is science, in the modern understanding of this word. I shall try to relate science and technology to some of the problems mentioned above. Science is the recognized darling of our day. Being a pragmatic people, we know it from its results — and these have been literally fantastic.

Science has fed us, clothed us, housed us as man has never been fed or clothed or housed before. Science has cured a thousand ills, given clear sight to the myopic, hearing to the deaf. Science has prolonged our lives, speeded our communications, given us wings to lengthen our travels. Science has simplified our housekeeping, has given us amusement at the touch of a button. Science has indeed brought close the ends of the earth, and is now vaulting the space beyond.

Who will dare to say that these are not good things? No one need say this, but it should be said that there are other good and even better things if man does not live by bread alone. Science is most truly valued when it is viewed in the total perspective of man's life and destiny, not as an exclusive blessing. A well-fed, well-clothed, well-housed man can be ignorant, prejudiced, and immoral too. A healthy man can be as unjust as an unhealthy man. A long life is not necessarily good or fruitful. Vastly expanded communications devices do not guarantee that much worthwhile is being communicated, and a world brought close together is not necessarily a world at peace. Simplified housekeeping does not guarantee happy marriages; easily accessible amusement cannot banish the boredom of a pointless life; and vitamins are no substitute for virtues.

What I am saying is that man has cherished many ennobling values; and that he stands to lose these if he allows himself to be seduced by the material benefits of science to the exclusion of the deep spiritual values that he cherished long before the advent of modern science and its accompanying technology. We can say this, and still be grateful for the blessings of science. But there is much more to the problem than this initial and superficial comment, particularly when we relate the position of science in the modern world to the cognate problem of university education in a world that is so enamored of science and so indebted to it.

The task of the university today, viewed in relation to its students, is twofold. The university must somehow transmit the intellectual and moral treasures of the past to its students, and, in doing this, must also somehow integrate this heritage with the new perspectives of the present and the future. The first aspect of the task is easier than the second. It is possible merely to speak nostalgically of the past as if the present and its own real problems and opportunities did not exist. It is equally possible to live completely in the present, as in an isolation ward, with no perception of our past heritage, its values and vital human meaning. I suspect that many departments of many universities are doing just one or another of these incomplete tasks and, in so doing, are failing to educate truly.

What is this past that is so often referred to as the culture of the West? It is no simple reality, but an amalgam of many elements. The main currents of influence can be identified, however. One finds at the base the great intellectual heritage that stems from the classical age of Greece. Here was the earliest root of the intellectual fibre of the West — the zest for universal understanding and philosophical inquiry, the joy of intellectual discovery, the deep appreciation for things of the spirit: truth, beauty, and the good. The Romans added another dimension to the tapestry of the West, the ideal of law and order, and a stable society of men with great civic institutions and an efficient administration of justice. Then there was the divine element of the Gospels, the fulfillment of the promise of the Old Testament, a new and bright light focused on man's nature and destiny, a fresh glimpse at the inner grandeur of the human person, new ideals of human thought, human achievement and high, indeed, eternal goals for human conduct. These three elements meshed to form what we know as Western culture. From this triple stock, we have derived that rich and complex heritage that is Western man's.

Whatever else man may become in the West in the years ahead, he will be poorer if, in his material progress, he loses the soul of his heritage which is centered in a concept of the human person as never fully understood before — glorying in the truth wherever and however it be found, strong and free under the law, cherishing art and beauty in its multitudious forms, living by the highest spiritual ideals of the Gospel, dedicated to eternal values for which he is also ready to die, indeed, better to die than to lose them. Respect for all that is uniquely man's, spirit, mind, freedom, truth, justice, beauty — the inner dignity of the human person — this is the heritage of the West that is ours to have and to hold and to teach.

But this is not a static heritage: Truth can have new expression and fuller understanding; justice, new causes to champion; beauty, new forms to inspire. Somehow the university must recomprehend, reinterpret, and reapply this heritage in every age. The heritage itself may become enriched and revitalized if this is done. If it is not done, the heritage may well become uninspiring, desiccated, devitalized, and even forgotten. Today science must be integrated as a part of this total heritage.

In a university context, the heritage is translated into many diverse disciplines: theology, philosophy, history, law, literature, language, economics, sociology, politics, mathematics, biology, physics, chemistry, geology, engineering. It is these latter, the physical sciences and their applications, that must be understood if they are to be integrated adequately into the rich heritage that antedated the present explosive development of the physical sciences. I know not where this integration can take place if not in a university — where all knowledge is communicated and extended in its totality and, one might hope, in proper perspective.

The focus of the university task is perhaps best seen in what it attempts to achieve in the minds and hearts of its students. We have often said at Notre Dame that whatever else we do, we attempt to give all our students the basic elements of a liberal education: one that will liberate the young student from the bondage of ignorance, prejudice, and passion. Our basic endeavor in every undergraduate college is the development to excellence of the student's use of his intelligence and freedom. A liberal education should enable the young man to form a reasonably complete and accurate concept of God, the world and man, some broad perception of man's situation and destiny in this world, and some inner realization of his relationship to God and to his fellow men. One would hope that all this would engender in the student some perspective and conviction so that the young man thus educated could direct his life in accordance with this total view of life's meaning. The really significant questions should be faced during this liberally

educative process, the live options should be thought-
fully and even prayerfully considered, so that the matur-
ing student is enabled to make, with an intelligence and
freedom worthy of man, the important and difficult
decisions that rational life demands. In summary, an
education worthy of the riches of our Western culture,
should somehow focus on the three great central realities
of nature, man, and God.

It is certainly understandable how difficult this task
of the University becomes in a world that is essentially
secularistic and scientifically oriented in its forward
march.

The cultural values of man and the eternal importance
of divine realities need not be lost or overshadowed in
such a world. But this has been the direction of recent
history: growing secularism, the divorce of the human
from the divine, the temporal from the eternal, the
material from the spiritual; and in the past century, the
nineteenth century scientists, in large numbers, declared
that God and revelation and religion were now irrelevant.

At this present juncture of history, our greatest challenge and opportunity is to understand both the vital importance of our heritage and the growing importance of
science, so that working together, instead of at cross
purposes, our heritage may be enriched and science may
become a fruitful instrument of man, not his master or
destroyer. How can this be done?

Science can be a powerful adjunct to the process of
liberal education that is at the heart of our mission, for
science, too, is one of the liberal arts. No person can be
liberally educated today without a reasonable grasp of
science and the great new vision of the universe, in its
innermost and outermost parts, that modern science has
brought us. The scientific method can also bring new and

imaginative and corrective insights into an educational process that was poorer without it. The student needs a respect for hard facts, accurately ascertained and expressed. Scientific curiosity, eagerness to postulate theoretical solutions and to verify them experimentally are worthy additions to mental maturity. Scientific speculation in the realms of pure science and mathematics prepares the student mentally for the more abstract studies of philosophy and theology which use intelligent reflection in another method of knowing to derive truths unattainable to physical science as such. Basic science and research may also engender in the student that respect for the mind at work which underlies all rational inquiry and human culture. Disrespect for the mind and the current sneering at intellectuals and intellectual endeavor is the quickest way to the destruction of all human culture. Scientific endeavor is finally a great school for discipline, for humility in the face of the yet unknown, for patience to work accurately, persistently and painstakingly — all real virtues and values in the process of a liberal education.

Science needs the other academic disciplines, too, for there is more to human life than the understanding and manipulation of nature. Science is power, and power needs direction to be meaningful. It is man who is the scientist, and science exists in the world of man. This world has total perspectives and man has a destiny beyond science. Science of itself cannot know God, or the nature of man, cannot establish justice, define morality, constitute culture or write poetry.

In the university, however, all of these things can be done and students can learn all that is true and valid regarding God, man, and nature. The same student can see the broad sweep of revealed truth in theology, and

the mind at work on ultimate problems in philosophy,
too; he can glory in the intuitive insights of poetry, thrill
at the recent discoveries of astrophysics, ponder the age-
old lessons of human success and failure in history and
literature. Perhaps the integration of all knowledge will
somehow come to existence in the mind of the student,
but how, except accidentally, if few of his professors
really understand or appreciate each other's specialized
branch of knowledge?

And how can all of the members of the academic
community come to some basic understanding and appreciation of the totality of knowledge unless there is a
continuing conversation among them on the points of
contact between the various disciplines that make up
the whole fabric of the universal knowledge?

I would not presume to outline such a conversation in
its totality, but it might be helpful to illustrate its possible
fruitfulness in one specific area most germane to what
we have already been considering.

It is common knowledge that the theologians and the
physicists have not been on speaking terms for centuries
— so much so that they no longer speak the same language. Their falling out was a classic case of misunderstanding and, unfortunately, the Galileo incident is still
regarded as a symbol of the presumed conflict between
science and faith.

The climate has now begun to change — and on both
sides. The time is ripe to take up a fruitful conversation
left aside centuries ago. The lead article in the most
recent issue of the best American Catholic theological
journal was on "The origin and age of the universe
appraised by science." Journals and bulletins of physicists
have begun to carry challenging articles of philosophical
and theological import. The physicists begin to sense a

broader responsibility to the world of nuclear fusion and fission that they have introduced to the brink of great good or great evil. As America's most renowned physicist said after Hiroshima and Nagasaki — the scientist has now known sin, a theological reality.

Much could be gained, I believe, by frankly discussing the conflicts of the past. One might, without too much difficulty, defend the position that most of the conflict has resulted from bad theology and bad science, too.

The fundamental error at the beginning, in the case of Galileo, was that the proper theological questions were not asked. The real theological question involved was how could this heliocentric doctrine of Copernicus and Galileo be squared with the fundamental Christian doctrine regarding the nature and destiny of man. Actually, there was and is no theological problem involved in the new theory. Instead of asking the proper theological question, however, the heliocentric system was viewed as opposed to a literal interpretation of the early chapters of Genesis, an interpretation which one of the greatest theologians, St. Augustine, would not have accepted centuries before Galileo, and which certainly no scriptural theologian of note would sustain today.

Our present Holy Father, Pius XII, in a recent message to the students of the Sorbonne clearly stated the case:

In your studies and scientific research rest assured that no contradiction is possible between certain truths of faith and established scientific facts. Nature, no less than revelation, proceeds from God and God cannot contradict Himself. Do not be dismayed if you hear the contrary affirmed insistently, even though research may have to wait for centuries to find the solution of the apparent opposition between science and faith.

Here in two brief phrases is the cause of most of the theologico-scientific disputes of the past: a misunderstanding of "the certain truths of faith" and "established scientific facts." Too often theologians have been all too little precise on what constituted "certain truths of faith." I say theologians, not the Church, which has been consistent and unchanging in its precise official statements of Catholic doctrine. And scientists, especially in the last century, were overconfident, to put it mildly, about "established scientific facts." You are aware of the utterly materialistic Victorian physicists who naively assumed the virtual finality, immutability, and even literal truth of their description of the nature of the world: the billiard ball models, Newton's laws of motion and gravitation, Hooke's law of elastic strain, and all the rest. Since then, we have seen centuries-old scientific views on matter, space and time summarily abandoned.

The latest theories are much more congenial to the corpus of Christian theological doctrine. But let us suppose that present scientific theories may again change in a way that may seem to challenge theological truth. Should this possiblity worry us? I think not, and I have no fears from science. Truth is our knowledge of what is, and given a fundamental unity of all that is, and different valid ways of knowing it, the seeming conflicts of today can merge into understanding tomorrow. Let us grant that there have been bad science and bad theology at times in the past. While the fundamental divinely revealed doctrines of the Church have never changed, theological understanding of them has progressed. Science, too, has progressed beyond false starts, and has learned to live with seemingly contradictory theories even within science itself — witness the history of scientific views on the theory of light. I am sure that theologians and physicists can live and work together fruitfully if they will only recognize the nature, the objectives, the limitations, and the methodological diversity of their different disciplines and share the quest along different paths for truth that is one. Science can learn things, such as the age of the earth, that theology as such cannot ever discover — given a lack of divine revelation on the subject. Theology, in turn, can know realities that are and always will be unknown to physical science as such: the notion of God and the good news of His economy of salvation for all the world and His promise of an eternal world to come.

Even Whitehead admitted that the notion of God was the greatest contribution of mediaeval theology to the formation of the scientific movement. You see, the theologian sees God not only as the Supreme Being of omnipotence and freedom, but also as the Source of rationality and order.

While God is free to create or not create a cosmos, and in choosing to create is free to create this cosmos or some other, when He did create this one, it was a cosmos, not a chaos, since it had to reflect His perfection and order. Because God is rational, His work is orderly, and because He is free, there is no predicting on our part as to just what this precise order will be. The world of Christian theism is then, at its foundation, a world congenial to empirical science with its twin method of observation and experiment. Unless there were regularities in this world, there would be nothing but chaos for science to discover, and because these are contingent regularities, they must be verified by experimentation.

One last word, and this one for the scientists. Who can measure the scientific effort and ingenuity that is expended on learning the few fragmentary scientific facts that we think we know right now for a certainty about the universe in its inner constitution and its outermost reaches? And yet, for the most part, scientists seem not too much concerned about the certain promise of divine revelation that for those who live and die in Christ, our Redeemer, there comes at the end of this earthly life the Blessed Vision of God Himself and, in God, all things will be known eternally and, to the limit of our finite powers, comprehensively as in their cause. If this be true, and Catholics everywhere are prepared to die for its truth and promise, then at least it deserves some investigation. I make a point of this, for one of my good scientist friends recently wrote that he knew nothing of immortality and couldn't be less interested. Even as a friend, apart from being a priest, I felt sad that he was spending so much time and energy for such meager gain while completely missing the chance to attain eternally a universal knowledge that is so much greater and more lasting.

So much for a suggested conversation between the physicists and theologians and its possible fruitfulness towards the integration of knowledge. I return, in conclusion, to our original point of departure, something for which we might fruitfully pray at the beginning of this new academic year: that each one of us might cherish the task of seeking and imparting truth in every way possible; that we disdain no truth, be it theological, philosophical, historical, poetic, or scientific; that we ourselves may be examples of the kinds of minds and hearts, the kinds of human persons whom we try to fashion by the educative process; and that we try to appreciate all that is good in the past while we bring its wisdom to bear in directing and giving ultimate meaning to the powerful forces that are awakening in our world today.

May God grant that this 115th year of our history will see us grow inwardly in wisdom, age, and grace, as we should, and may the University grow with us, as it most certainly will not grow without us.

CPSIA information can be obtained
at www.ICGtesting.com
Printed in the USA
LVHW081511260122
709472LV00026B/221